Glory, Glory, How Peculiar

Prentice-Hall, Inc.
Englewood Cliffs / New Jersey

compiled by
Charles Keller

Glory, Glory, How Peculiar

illustrated by
Lady McCrady

For Coby, Bayard, Paul and Jackie

Prentice-Hall International, Inc., London
Prentice-Hall of Australia, Pty. Ltd., North Sydney
Prentice-Hall of Canada, Ltd., Toronto
Prentice-Hall of India Private Ltd., New Delhi
Prentice-Hall of Japan, Inc., Tokyo

Library of Congress Cataloging in Publication Data

Glory, glory, how peculiar.

    Children's songs.
    Includes index.
    SUMMARY: A collection of humorous songs set to
old, familiar tunes.
    1. Children's songs. [1. Songs] I. Keller,
Charles II. McCrady, Lady.
M1997.G58   784.6'24   76-10171

ISBN 0-13-357392-3

Table of Contents

Glory, Glory, How Peculiar

Mine eyes have seen the glo ry Of the

downfall of the school. We have bothered all the teachers, we've

brok en ev' ry rule. We tore in to the of fice And we

tickled the principal. Our truth is marching on.

Glo ry, glo ry, how pe cu liar. Teach er hit me with a

rul er, Cause I bopped her on the bean with a

rot ten tan·ger ine, And the juice came running down.

Tune: Battle Hymn of the Republic

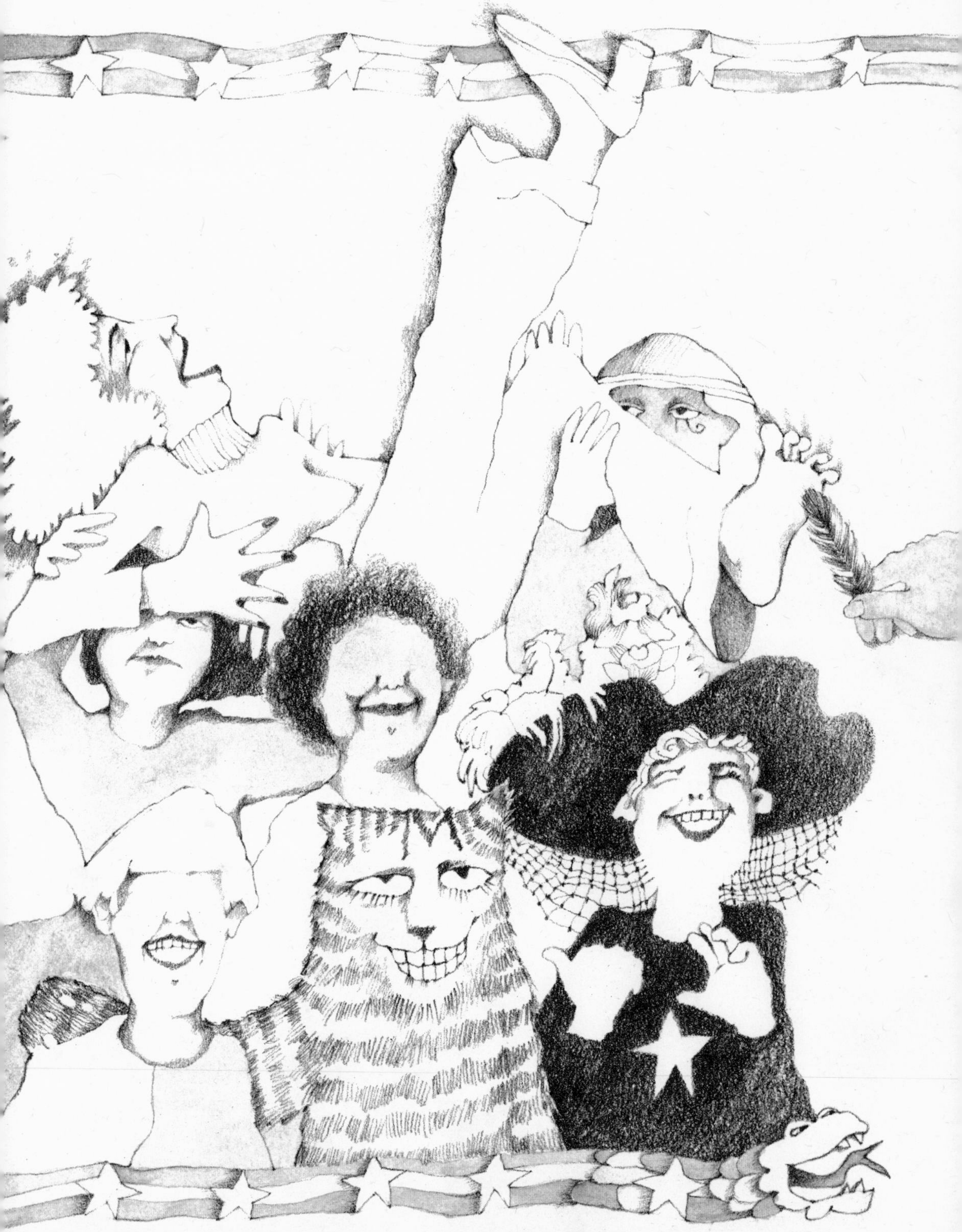

Found A Peanut

Found a peanut, found a peanut Found a peanut   last

night Last night I found a peanut Found a peanut last night.

Broke it open, broke it open
Broke it open last night
Last night I broke it open
Broke it open last night.

It was rotten, it was rotten

Ate it anyway, ate it anyway

Got a tummyache, got a tummyache

Called the doctor, called the doctor

Appendicitis, appendicitis

Operation, operation

Died anyway, died anyway

Went to heaven, went to heaven

Didn't want me, didn't want me

Went the other way, Went the other way

Wouldn't take me, wouldn't take me

Stayed anyway, stayed anyway

Shovelled coal, shovelled coal

Burnt my thumb, burnt my thumb

It was a dream, it was a dream
It was a dream last night
Last night it was a dream
It was a dream last night.

Tune: Clementine

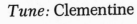

Neath the Crust
Of the Old Apple Pie

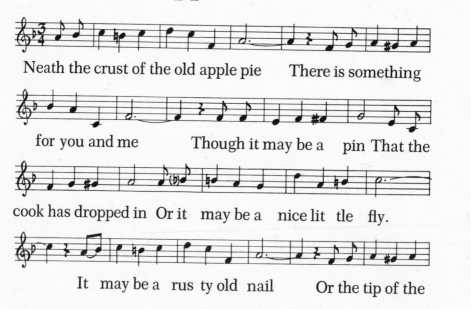

Neath the crust of the old apple pie   There is something

for you and me   Though it may be a   pin That the

cook has dropped in   Or it   may be a   nice lit tle   fly.

It may be a rus ty old nail   Or the tip of the

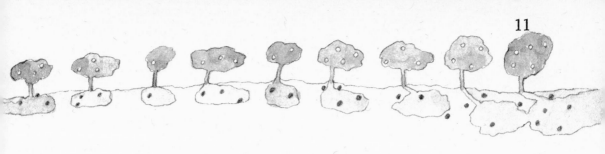

pus sy-cat tail But whatev er it be It's for

you and for me Neath the crust of the old apple pie.

Tune: In the Shade of the Old Apple Tree

In Frisco Bay

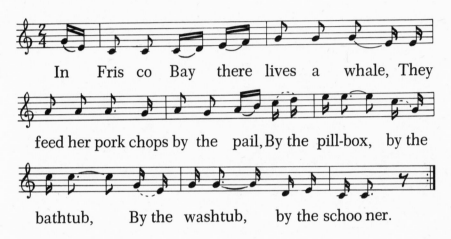

In Fris co Bay there lives a whale, They

feed her pork chops by the pail, By the pill-box, by the

bathtub, By the washtub, by the schoo ner.

Her name is Sarah, and she's a peach,
But don't leave food within her reach,
Or nursemaids, or babies,
Or chocolate ice-cream sodas.

She loves to eat and when she smiles
You can see her teeth for miles and miles,
And spare ribs, and tonsils,
And things too fierce to mention.

Now what would you do in a case like that?
Now what would you do but step on your hat,
Or your mother, or your toothbrush,
Or anything else that's helpless?

Tune: Dixie

We Three Kings

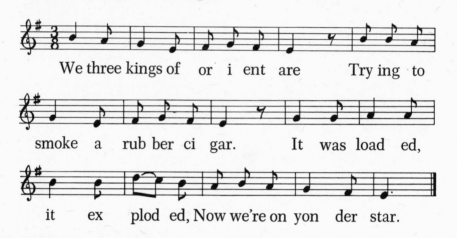

We three kings of or i ent are   Try ing to

smoke a rub ber ci gar.   It was load ed,

it   ex   plod ed, Now we're on yon der star.

Tune: We Three Kings

Ford Song

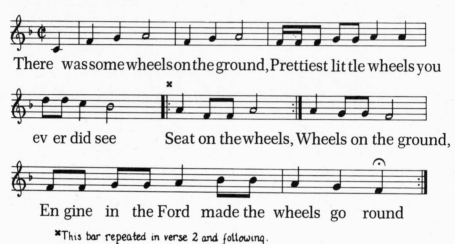

There was some wheels on the ground, Prettiest lit tle wheels you

ev er did see   Seat on the wheels, Wheels on the ground,

En gine in the Ford made the wheels go round

*This bar repeated in verse 2 and following.

On the wheels there was a seat,
Prettiest little seat you ever did see
Seat on the wheels,
Wheels on the ground,
Engine in the Ford made the wheels go round

And on the seat there was a girl

And on the girl there was a hat

And on the hat there was a feather

And on the feather there was a flea

And on the flea there was a spot,
Prettiest little spot you ever did see
Spot on the flea,
Flea on the feather,
Feather on the hat,
Hat on the girl,
Girl on the seat,
Seat on the wheels,
Wheels on the ground,
Engine in the Ford made the wheels go round

Tune: Green Grass Grows All Around

Do Your Ears Hang Low

Do your ears hang low Do they wobble to and fro Can you

tie them in a knot Can you tie them in a bow? Can you

throw them over your shoulder The way you used to do? Do your ears hang low?

Tune: Turkey In the Straw

D-A-V-E-N-P
O-R-T spells Davenport, Davenport
That's the only decent kind of love seat, love seat
The guy that made it must have been a
heart beat, heart beat.
D-A-V-E-N-P-O-R-T for me
It's a hug and a squeeze and an "Oh Henry, please,"
That's Davenport for me.

Lollipop

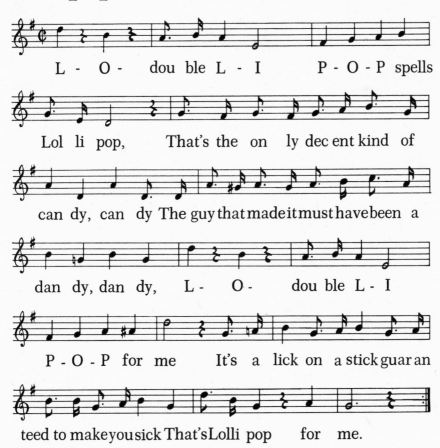

L - O - dou ble L - I   P - O - P spells

Lol li pop,   That's the on ly dec ent kind of

can dy, can dy The guy that made it must have been a

dan dy, dan dy,   L- O-   dou ble L - I

P - O - P for me   It's a lick on a stick guar an

teed to make you sick That's Lolli pop   for me.

Tune: Harrigan

On Top of Spaghetti

On top of spa ghet ti   All covered with cheese,

I lost my poor meatball When somebody sneezed.

It rolled off the table
And on to the floor,
And then my poor meatball
It rolled out the door.

And early next summer
It grew into a tree,
All covered with meatballs
All ready for me.

It rolled into the garden
And under a bush,
And then my poor meatball
Was nothing but mush.

So if you eat spaghetti
All covered with cheese,
Hold on to your meatball
And don't ever sneeze.

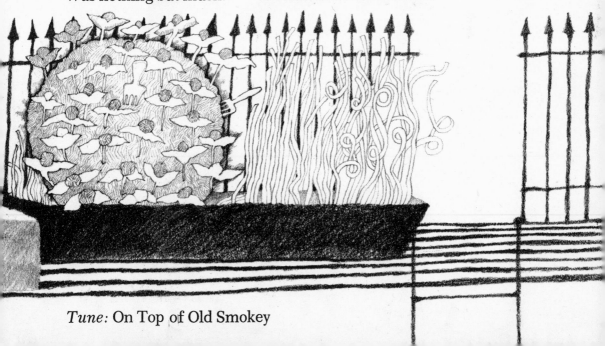

Tune: On Top of Old Smokey

The Ants Come Marching One By One

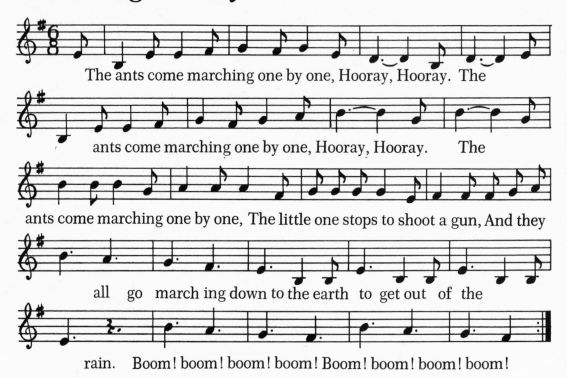

The ants come marching one by one, Hooray, Hooray. The

ants come marching one by one, Hooray, Hooray.   The

ants come marching one by one, The little one stops to shoot a gun, And they

all go march ing down to the earth to get out of the

rain.   Boom! boom! boom! boom! Boom! boom! boom! boom!

The ants come marching two by two,
The little one stops to tie his shoe.

The ants come marching three by three,
The little one stops to climb a tree.

The ants come marching four by four,
The little one stops to close the door.

The ants come marching five by five,
The little one stops to wave good-bye.

The ants come marching six by six,
The little one stops to pick up sticks.

The ants come marching seven by seven,
The little one stops to look at heaven.

The ants come marching eight by eight,
The little one stops to shut the gate.

The ants come marching nine by nine,
The little one stops to tell the time.

The ants come marching ten by ten,
The little one stops to say *The End.*

Tune: When Johnny Comes Marching Home

Long Nail A-Grinding

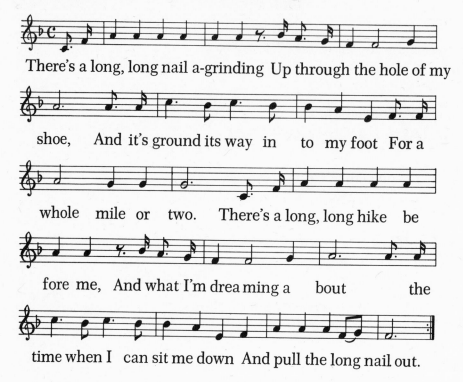

There's a long, long nail a-grinding Up through the hole of my

shoe,   And it's ground its way in   to my foot For a

whole   mile   or   two.   There's a long, long hike   be

fore me,   And what I'm drea ming a   bout   the

time when I   can sit me down And pull the long nail out.

The fish it never cackles 'bout
Its million eggs or so,
The hen is quite a different bird
One egg—and hear her crow.

The fish we spurn, but crown the hen
Which leads me to surmise,
Don't hide your light, but blow your horn,
It pays to advertise.

Tune: There's a Long, Long Trail A-Winding

Cow on the Railroad Track

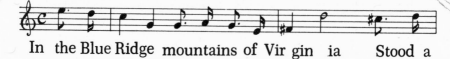

In the Blue Ridge mountains of Vir gin ia   Stood a

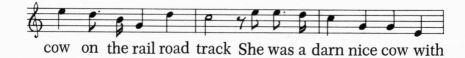

cow on the rail road track She was a darn nice cow with

eyes so kind But a cow can't read a railroad sign.

So she stood in the middle of the track
And the train gave her a whack on the back—
Now you'll find her horns in old Virginia
And her tail on the lonesome track.

(YELL!)

S—P—I—N—E   Backbone!

Tune: The Trail of the Lonesome Pine

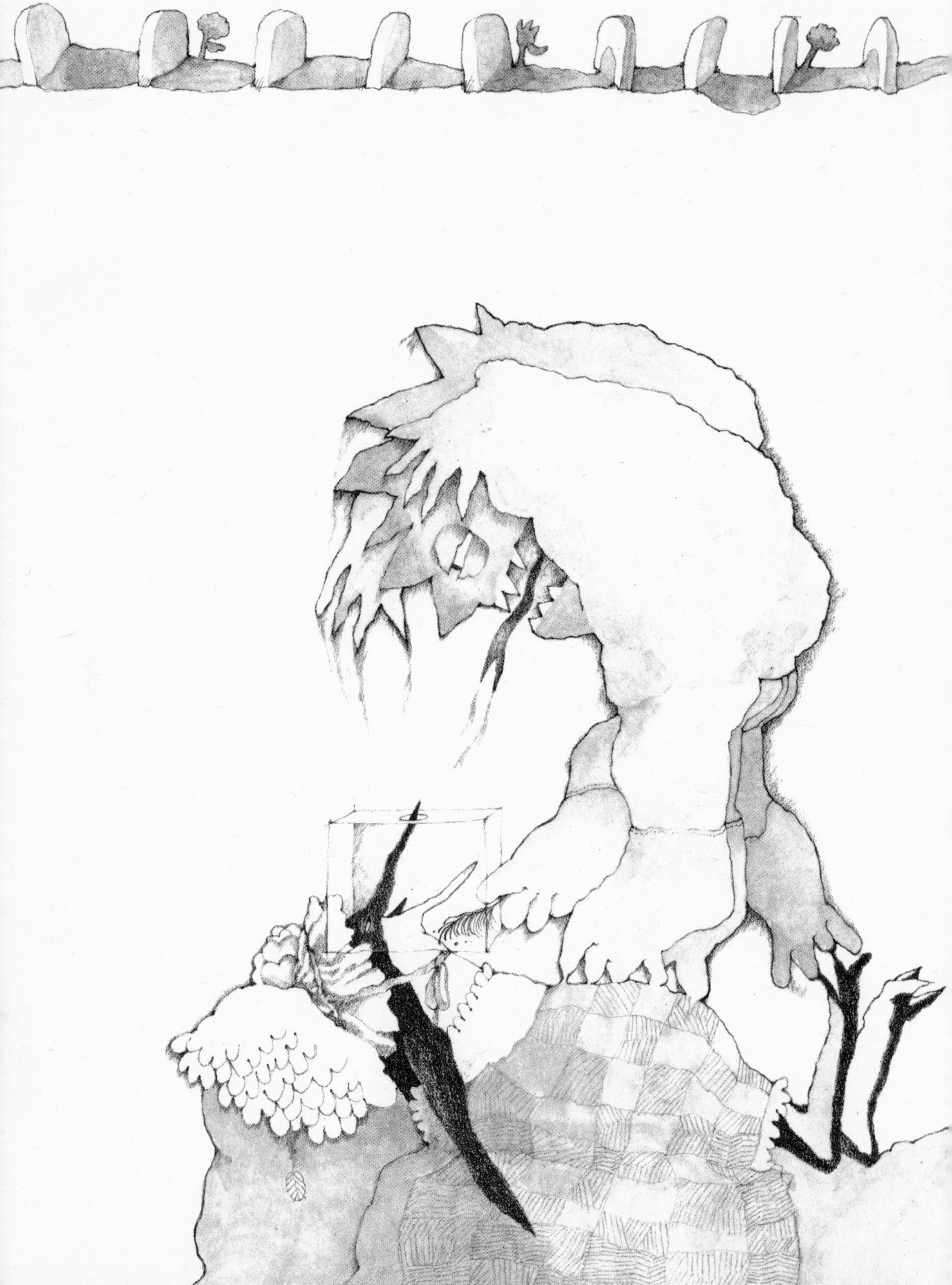

John Brown's Baby

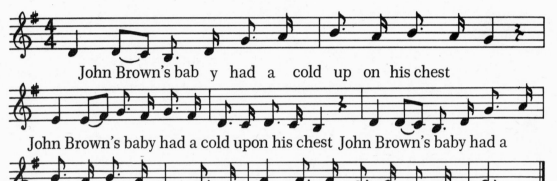

John Brown's bab y had a cold up on his chest

John Brown's baby had a cold upon his chest John Brown's baby had a

cold upon his chest And they cured it with camphorated oil.

Tune: John Brown's Body

Web-Footed Friends

Be kind to your web-footed friend, For that duck may be

somebody's broth   er,   He lives in the midst of a

swamp,   Where it's awfully cold and   damp,

Now you may think that this is the end, Well it is!

Tune: Stars and Stripes Forever

GOODBYE